CRIME SCENE INVESTIGATOR

By Geoffrey M. Horn

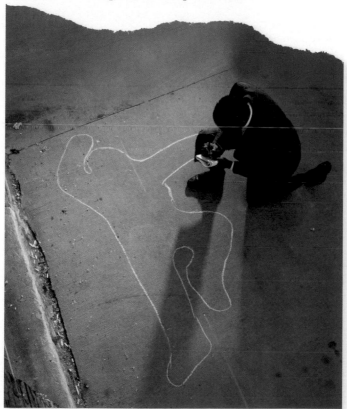

Reading Consultant: Susan Nations, M.Ed.,
author/literacy coach/consultant in literacy development

Gareth Stevens
Publishing

Please visit our web site at **www.garethstevens.com**.
For a free catalog describing Gareth Stevens Publishing's list of high-quality books, call 1-800-542-2595 (USA) or 1-800-387-3178 (Canada).
Gareth Stevens Publishing's fax: 1-877-542-2596

Library of Congress Cataloging-in-Publication Data

Horn, Geoffrey M.
    Crime scene investigator / by Geoffrey M. Horn.
        p. cm.—(Cool careers, adventure careers)
    Includes bibliographical references and index.
    ISBN-10: 0-8368-8880-4   ISBN-13: 978-0-8368-8880-5 (lib. bdg.)
    ISBN-10: 0-8368-8887-1   ISBN-13: 978-0-8368-8887-4 (softcover)
    1. Forensic sciences—Vocational guidance—Juvenile literature.   2. Criminal investigation—Vocational guidance—Juvenile literature.   3. Criminal investigation—Juvenile literature.   I. Title.
    HV8073.8.H67   2008
    363.25'2—dc22   2007026984

This edition first published in 2008 by
Gareth Stevens Publishing
A Weekly Reader® Company
1 Reader's Digest Road
Pleasantville, NY 10570-7000 USA

Copyright © 2008 by Gareth Stevens, Inc.

Senior Managing Editor: Lisa M. Guidone
Managing Editor: Valerie J. Weber
Creative Director: Lisa Donovan
Designer: Paula Jo Smith
Cover Photo Researcher: Kimberly Babbitt
Interior Photo Researcher: Susan Anderson

Picture credits: Cover, title page, Superstock; pp. 4–5 © Ashley Cooper/Corbis; pp. 6–7 Robert Voets CBS/Getty Images; p. 9 Scott Olson/Getty Images; p. 10 Stephen Aaron Rees/Shutterstock; p. 11 Shutterstock; p. 13 © BLUESTAR®; pp. 14–15 Charles Dharapak/AP; p. 16 Graeme Robertson/Getty Images; p. 19 Steve Liss/Getty Images; p. 20 Jason Hunt/AP; pp. 22–23 Veer; pp. 24–25 Superstock; p. 26 Aijaz Rahi/AP; p. 29 Elise Amendola/AP

Printed in the United States of America

1 2 3 4 5 6 7 8 9 10 09 08 07

CONTENTS

Words in the glossary appear in **bold** type the first time they are used in the text.

CHAPTER 1

ON THE SCENE

P olice have many ways to fight crime. Guns, cars, trucks, motorcycles — a big-city police force uses these tools every day. But sometimes it doesn't take weapons or high-speed vehicles to catch criminals. Sometimes all it takes is a broken car door handle.

Getting a Handle on Crime

The broken handle was a clue in an actual case in Los Angeles, California. Thieves stole a safe and drove it to a wooded area. They used **explosives** to blow the safe open. Then they took the valuable items from inside the safe.

When the crime was reported, specially trained officers were sent to the scene. These special police were crime scene investigators — the **CSI** team. The team made a complete search of the crime scene. That's when they discovered the car door handle.

Later, a suspect in the case was arrested. The suspect owned a car — with a missing door handle. The handle from the crime scene matched the car door exactly. The suspect made a full **confession.**

Behind crime scene tape, a CSI team looks for clues to crack a murder case.

Different Words for the Same Job

Students who want to become crime scene investigators often take courses in forensic science. The term *forensic* comes from a Latin word that means "related to the law." A **forensic scientist** is someone who uses science to solve crimes.

Risks and Rewards

Crime scene investigators solve many different kinds of crimes, including murder. CSI work can be tough, but it is also very rewarding. As a member of a CSI team, you need a keen eye, a good mind, and a strong stomach. You can be called to a crime scene at any hour of the day or night. A dead body can look awful and smell worse. You see the worst things that one person can do to another.

Why choose CSI as a career? "Each day when I go to work, I feel like an adventure awaits me," said CSI worker Laura Santos. CSI team members share the excitement of solving hard cases. They help put criminals behind bars. They also help clear people who were accused of crimes that they did not do. Police who do CSI work may carry guns and face dangerous criminals. But most of today's CSI workers catch crooks with lab tests instead of weapons.

Emily Procter plays Detective Calleigh Duquesne on the hit TV series *CSI: Miami.*

Do the CSI TV Shows Get It Right?

Each week, millions of people watch CSI programs on TV. The original series *CSI: Crime Scene Investigation* is set in Las Vegas, Nevada. A second series takes place in Miami, Florida. A third happens in New York City.

Like a real-life CSI team, the TV investigators use science to solve crimes. But they also do things a real-life CSI team could never do. For example, the TV team can solve two murder cases in less than an hour. In real life, cases can take weeks — even months — to solve.

Here's another example of how TV differs from real life. In one CSI show, a member of the CSI team thinks a **serial killer** is targeting him. He goes to the suspect's home alone. The scene makes for good TV drama. But it's a risk no real-life investigator would take.

CHAPTER 2
LOOKING FOR CLUES

There are many different kinds of crimes and many different kinds of crime scenes. For a robbery, the crime scene might be a bank. For a mugging, the crime scene might be a dark alley. For a hit-and-run accident, the crime scene might be a busy street. A crime scene can be small, like the backseat of a car. Or it can be huge, like a bombed building.

Sizing Up the Crime Scene

Most cases begin with a call to 911. The 911 operator alerts nearby patrol cars. Soon, police in uniform arrive. If the victim needs help, they provide it. Sometimes they see a clear suspect. If so, they may make a quick arrest. They also keep people away from the crime scene until the CSI team arrives.

The main job of the CSI team is to "process" the crime scene. One investigator says the first thing she likes to do is make a "mental picture" of the scene. If there is a body, where is it? Any bloodstains? Fingerprint smudges? Evidence of a struggle? Are any people present besides the police? How do they look? How are they behaving?

Taking photos is an important part of "processing" a crime scene. The photos can later be used as evidence at a trial.

The CSI team uses tape, rope, and barriers to mark off the crime scene. Sometimes it takes a while to decide how big the crime scene really is. Suppose the team is called to investigate a break-in on a rainy evening. The home's owners say their diamond jewelry has been stolen.

The crime scene starts out as the room where the jewels were kept. Then the investigator notices muddy footprints on the floor. The footprints lead across the room to an open window. From there, footprints are found going through a flower garden to a driveway. The crime scene now includes the outside as well as the inside of the house.

After a break-in, a muddy footprint can show the kind of shoe the burglar wore, how much the thief weighs, and whether the lawbreaker was walking or running.

The footprints may offer valuable clues to the kind of boots or shoes the thief wore. They may show how much the thief weighs. If the driveway also is muddy, tire tracks can provide key evidence.

Dusting for Prints

All people have tiny ridges on the tips of their fingers. The patterns made by these ridges form fingerprints. No two people have the same prints — not even identical twins.

When people get sweat, grease, dirt, or blood on their fingers, they leave print marks on anything they touch. The best way to avoid leaving print marks is to wear gloves. (This is why members of the CSI team wear gloves when handling evidence. They do not want to add their fingerprints to the crime scene.)

Sometimes prints are easily seen as smudges. More often, the prints are hidden, or **latent.** Investigators use special powders and brushes to "dust" for latent prints. The dust patterns reveal the prints clearly under special kinds of light.

Police departments keep fingerprint files. The **Federal Bureau of Investigation (FBI)** has a computer file with more than 40 million sets of prints. Years ago, it took months to finish a fingerprint check. Today, prints found at a crime scene can be matched with those of a known criminal in less than two hours.

The CSI Kit

A crime scene investigator always needs a fully stocked kit. Among many other things, a CSI kit holds:

- Gloves
- A flashlight
- Bags, cans, and boxes to hold evidence
- Tags to label the evidence
- Fingerprint powders and brushes
- **Luminol** to reveal traces of blood
- A magnifying glass
- Scissors and tweezers
- A knife for scraping dried materials
- Tubes for collecting blood samples
- Swabs for taking **DNA** samples
- A sketchpad, writing paper, and pens

Was this bathtub the scene of a bloody crime? Luminol's telltale glow may help solve the mystery.

At the crime scene, one or more investigators collect evidence. Others shoot photos and videos of everything they find. Even the smallest bit of evidence can be important. For example, a cigarette butt found at a murder scene could have the killer's fingerprints or DNA.

What Is Luminol?

Suppose you're part of a CSI team. You find a body dumped in the woods. You think the victim might have been stabbed to death in a nearby cabin. You go to the cabin and look around, but you see no blood. Did the killer scrub the walls and floor to erase any signs of struggle?

One way to find out is to use luminol. This chemical can detect even the tiniest traces of blood. CSI teams carry luminol in a spray bottle mixed with water and other chemicals. When luminol comes in contact with blood, it glows. The outline of a stain can be seen clearly for thirty seconds or more.

Luminol is not perfect. Sometimes it reacts where there is no blood. For example, it glows when it touches bleach. But it remains an important part of the CSI kit.

CHAPTER 3

AT THE CRIME LAB

E very bit of evidence found at a crime scene is bagged and tagged. Some of it is sent to the crime lab for further testing. Every CSI team relies on good lab work.

Fighting Crimes With Science

Crime lab workers don't carry guns. They don't catch crooks in high-speed chases. They rarely meet the criminals they put in jail. But their work can be both exciting and important.

Early crime labs studied fingerprints. A system for analyzing prints was developed in Great Britain in the 1890s. London's police force at Scotland Yard opened its first fingerprint office in 1901. Today, its crime lab is still one of the world's best.

The FBI crime lab was founded in 1932. In its first year, it carried out 963 tests. Now it conducts more than 1 million tests yearly. Over the years, the FBI lab has added many tools to help CSI workers. The crime lab set up its first DNA unit in 1988.

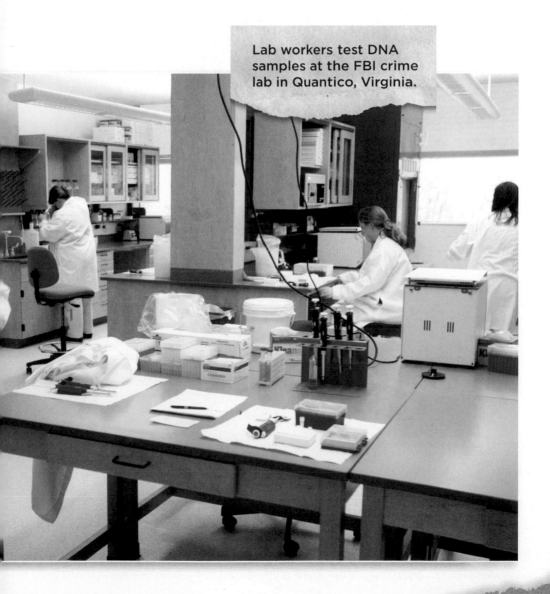

Lab workers test DNA samples at the FBI crime lab in Quantico, Virginia.

Investigating a stabbing case in London, England, a CSI team carefully labels even the smallest clues.

Tracing a Killer

It's easy to see the big things at a crime scene, like a body. But the CSI team must also be on the lookout for very small things, such as bits of paint or fabric. Such materials are called **trace evidence.** Trace evidence is usually sent to a crime lab. There, trained lab workers use microscopes and other tools to study it.

Small things can tell a big story. Suppose someone has been run over by a hit-and-run driver. Bits of paint on or around the victim can help show the kind of car the driver used. Bits of fiber from the victim's clothing may have stuck to the bottom of the car. They, too, can be used as evidence.

What Is DNA Testing?

DNA is the substance that tells your body how to grow. It is found in every cell in your body. Your DNA determines your sex, race, and height. Your hair and eye color also depend on your DNA. Identical twins share the same DNA. Everyone else's DNA is different.

Suppose you're part of a CSI team investigating a murder. It looks as if the victim tried to fight off the killer. You might find bits of the killer's skin under the victim's fingernails. You could then send the skin samples to a lab for DNA testing. The result could be compared to the DNA of the main suspects in the case. It could also be compared to the DNA of known criminals in police files.

DNA evidence is very powerful. It can be used at a trial to **convict** a killer. It can also be used to free people who have been unfairly accused. Recently, some people sentenced to death have been freed. Tests showed that their DNA did not match the DNA found at the crime scene.

Gun Crimes

In murder cases, guns are the most common weapons. In 2005, handguns were used to kill 55 percent of all murder victims. Rifles, shotguns, and other types of guns killed another 16 percent of the victims.

The study of guns and bullets is called **ballistics.** Bullets found at a crime scene may be sent to a ballistics lab for further study. The first crime lab in the United States was a ballistics lab. It was started in Los Angeles in 1923.

Was the same gun that fired these bullets used to commit a crime? That's the question this ballistics expert for the Washington, D.C., police is trying to answer.

After a gun is fired, traces of gunpowder may stay on a shooter's hands or clothes for up to six hours. This trace evidence is called **gunshot residue,** or **GSR.** Samples from a suspect's hands or clothes can be sent to the lab for GSR testing. This kind of testing has limits. It may not work if shooters washed their hands. And the lab can't prove a suspect fired a particular gun. But it can prove someone handled a gun or was near one when it fired.

Learning From Bullets

The inside of a gun barrel is not smooth. Instead, it has grooves that form a spiral pattern. These grooves make the bullet's flight more accurate. They also leave marks on the bullet.

Different guns have different groove patterns. Using a microscope, ballistics experts can study the groove marks left on a bullet. These marks will tell them whether the bullet might have come from a particular gun. Experts can also find out whether two or more bullets came from the same gun.

CHAPTER 4
DEAD CERTAIN

Each day, on average, more than 6,500 people die in the United States. Most die of natural causes. Accidents kill about 300 people a day. Another 100 or so commit suicide. About 50 people each day are murdered.

When police are called to a death scene, the first question they try to answer is, How did the person die?

Along with the CSI team, emergency medical workers arrive at the scene of an accident.

Finding the Cause

Suppose you're a member of a CSI team. You need to decide what caused a person's death. Was it an accident, suicide — or murder? People who knew the dead person may be very upset. You understand the pain they may be going through. But you can't let their feelings — or yours — stop you from doing your job.

The first clues you probably look for are signs of a fight. Do you see lots of bloodstains? Broken glass? Overturned chairs? Bloody handprints on doorknobs, chair legs, or telephones may also be signs of a struggle. Wounds on the victim's hands and arms are even clearer signs. He or she might have been resisting the murderer.

You look closely at the body. Do you see any bullet holes? Knife wounds? Other kinds of wounds? Based on what you find, the CSI team can then begin searching for a weapon.

Preparing for a CSI Career

In 2005, the United States had about 11,000 CSI workers. On average, they earned more than $21 an hour. The need for CSI workers is growing.

CSI workers need a strong science background. They must also take college courses in criminal justice.

Taking a Closer Look

You've decided. You're sure this is a murder case. But your feeling is only the first step in a long process. Investigators continue to go over the crime scene. Meanwhile, another member of the CSI team — the **pathologist** — begins to examine the body. A pathologist is a doctor who studies the effects of disease and death.

In the lab, the pathologist and other CSI members take an even closer look at the body. This very detailed exam is called an **autopsy.** First, CSI team members check the skin for scars and tattoos. They take trace evidence from clothing and fingernails. They check the hands for gunshot residue. Next, the body is cleaned and laid out on a steel table.

Then, the pathologist cuts open the body. Many kinds of evidence may lie inside. **Tissues** and organs may be tested. They can show whether the victim took drugs, drank alcohol, or was given poison. If the victim has been shot, the pathologist will try to show the path each bullet took through the body.

Dental X-rays do more than help a dentist take care of your teeth. They also help CSI teams identify the bodies of murder victims.

Taking a Bite Out of Crime

Everyone's mouth is different. Some people are missing teeth. Others have chipped, cracked, or crooked teeth. Teeth and dental work are often preserved even in bodies that are badly damaged or decayed. The CSI team can take photos of the teeth. They can then compare the photos with dentists' X-rays to find out who the dead person was.

In 2005, the FBI began setting up a new national center for dental records. This should make it much easier for CSI teams to identify missing persons.

CHAPTER 5

CRIME SCENE CHAOS

I magine a crime scene so large it covers whole sections of a city. Fires rage out of control. Hundreds of people are injured or killed. It sounds like a horror movie. But horrors like these have actually happened. Riots and **terrorism** have tested the skills and courage of CSI teams around the globe.

Riots in Los Angeles

On March 3, 1991, California police stopped Rodney King after a high-speed chase. King, an African American, was ordered out of the car. The police say King began behaving oddly. Four officers then hit him with their batons. The scene was caught on video and shown all over the world.

Riots in April 1992 turned parts of Los Angeles, California, into a huge crime scene.

Charged with beating King, the four officers were put on trial. In April 1992, the jury reached

a verdict — not guilty. Black neighborhoods in Los Angeles erupted in fury. The riots lasted four days. Fifty-five people were killed. Businesses were looted. Buildings were burned.   About two thousand people were hurt, and twelve thousand were arrested. The riot areas became one of the biggest crime scenes in U.S. history.

Terror in Mumbai

Like riots, terrorism can create huge crime scenes. In Mumbai, India, seven terrorist bombs killed more than two hundred people on July 11, 2006. The bombs were planted on seven different trains. They all blew up between 6:24 and 6:35 P.M., during the evening rush hour.

Police at Mahim station in Mumbai, India, investigate one of the seven trains bombed by terrorists in 2006.

Police at the crime scene had to brave difficult and dangerous conditions. The next day, CSI teams began moving **debris** from the trains to a railroad yard. Investigators needed to find out how the bombs were made. They also needed to stop the terrorist group that carried out the attacks. The safety of everyone in the whole city would depend on how well this CSI team did its work.

The Bomb Squad

For CSI workers, a bomb that has already gone off isn't the biggest threat. An even bigger danger is a bomb that hasn't gone off — yet. Unexploded bombs may be booby-trapped. Some bombs have motion detectors. These devices sense movement and can blow up and kill anyone who comes too close.

Anytime an unexploded bomb is found, the bomb squad is called in. Members of the bomb squad have special training to dispose of bombs safely. They also use special equipment, including robots. Even so, bomb squad members have a very dangerous job. Many have been wounded or killed.

Throughout the world, terrorists sometimes use a cruel strategy. They set off one bomb in a marketplace, killing dozens of people. Then, a short while later, they set off a second bomb. This second bomb is designed to kill police, CSI teams, doctors, and other first responders.

Heroes at Ground Zero

Terror struck the United States on September 11, 2001. The worst attack came in New York City. Two hijacked airplanes smashed into the twin towers of the World Trade Center. A terrible fire raged, and the two buildings collapsed. About twenty-eight hundred people died at the scene. The site is now known as Ground Zero.

In the weeks after the attack, many CSI volunteers came to Ground Zero. These heroes had to wade through many thousands of tons of twisted steel and crushed concrete. At first, the teams tried to find survivors. Then they worked to identify the dead.

One of the CSI volunteers was Dr. Paula Brumit. Dr. Brumit, a dentist, came to New York from Texas in April 2002. By then, parts of bodies were being stored in twenty thousand bags. Using dental records, she was able to identify several victims. One was a firefighter; another was a police officer. In one case, all she had to go on was a single tooth. She showed that good CSI work can solve even the deepest crime scene mysteries.

Facing page: Eighteen days after terrorists destroyed the World Trade Center, workers at Ground Zero continued to search for survivors — and for clues.

GLOSSARY

autopsy — a detailed examination of a dead body to determine how someone died

ballistics — the science of guns and bullets

confession — a statement that someone gives admitting that he or she did the crime

convict — to find or prove guilty of a crime

CSI — short for "crime scene investigation"

debris — the remains of something that has been broken down or destroyed

DNA — a substance that is found in all living things that determines their traits

explosives — devices that explode, destroying nearby objects and areas

Federal Bureau of Investigation (FBI) — the U.S. government's main crime-fighting agency

forensic scientist — someone who uses science to solve crimes; another term for a crime scene investigator

gunshot residue (GSR) — the traces of gunpowder that remain on a shooter's hands or clothing after firing a gun

latent — hidden

luminol — a chemical that can detect tiny bits of blood

pathologist — a doctor who studies the effects of disease and death on the body

serial killer — a criminal who, over time, murders several people in a similar way

terrorism — the use of violence to force people (or their government) to meet certain demands

tissues — in medicine, the groups of cells that make up parts of the body

trace evidence — evidence found at a crime scene in very small amounts, such as paint chips or fibers

TO FIND OUT MORE

Books

Batman's Guide to Crime and Detection. DK Readers Series. Michael Teitelbaum (DK Publishing)

Crime Scene Detective: Using Science and Critical Thinking to Solve Crimes. Karen Schulz (Prufrock Press)

Crime Scene: How Investigators Use Science to Track Down the Bad Guys. Vivien Bowers (Maple Tree Press)

Crime-Solving Science Projects: Forensic Science Experiments. Kenneth G. Rainis (Enslow Publishers)

Detective Science: 40 Crime-Solving, Case-Breaking, Crook-Catching Activities for Kids. Jim Wiese (Jossey-Bass)

The Master Detective Handbook: Help Our Detectives Use Gadgets & Super Sleuthing Skills to Solve the Mystery & Catch the Crooks. Janice Eaton Kilby (Lark Books)

When Objects Talk: Solving a Crime With Science. Mark P. Friedlander, Jr., and Terry M. Phillips (Lerner Publications)

Web Sites

CBS.com: CSI
www.cbs.com/primetime/csi
   Check out the official site of the "CSI" TV show.

Crime Scene Investigation
www.crime-scene-investigator.net/index.html
   Find out what it takes to become a member of a CSI team.

Federal Bureau of Investigation: Kids' Page
www.fbi.gov/fbikids.htm
   Learn how the FBI does its work.

Publisher's note to educators and parents: Our editors have carefully reviewed these web sites to ensure that they are suitable for children. Many web sites change frequently, however, and we cannot guarantee that a site's future contents will continue to meet our high standards of quality and educational value. Be advised that children should be closely supervised whenever they access the Internet.

INDEX

About the Author

Geoffrey M. Horn has written more than three dozen books for young people and adults, along with hundreds of articles for encyclopedias and other works. He lives in southwestern Virginia, in the foothills of the Blue Ridge Mountains, with his wife, their collie, and six cats. He dedicates this book to Valerie Weber, Tammy West, Diane Laska-Swanke, and the rest of the Milwaukee creative team.